READER'S COMMENTS

"After Bill Eddy gave a statewide seminar to our family court judges in 2005, I received the highest ratings ever on our feedback forms. His knowledge and examples as an experienced lawyer and therapist were extremely helpful to them. He went beyond just explaining the problem (as many speakers do) and offered many specific tools to manage these parties. **Managing High Conflict People in Court** *provides these tools in a nutshell."*

Megan Hunter, MBA
Vice President, High Conflict Institute
Former Family Law Specialist, Administrative
Office of the Courts, Arizona Supreme Court

"As a frequent trainer of family law judges and attorneys, I find Mr. Eddy's book to be an excellent resource for judges and attorneys. Bill Eddy captures the critical components of Cluster B personality disorders and teaches how they often contribute to the high conflict population."

Philip Stahl, Ph.D.
Author of "Parenting After Divorce"

*"***Managing High Conflict People in Court*** is not a dry, academic text, but a succinct, highly pragmatic, and extremely useful tool for Judges and court personnel to understand, and cope with high conflict people in court, thereby having more* **orderly,** *effective,* and **fair** *court hearings, for all parties to the dispute."*

Judge Sol Gothard, JD, MSW, ACSW
Fifth Circuit Court of Appeal, LA (ret)

T0126318

MANAGING
HIGH CONFLICT
PEOPLE IN COURT

MANAGING HIGH CONFLICT PEOPLE IN COURT

By Bill Eddy, LCSW, ESQ.

MANAGING HIGH CONFLICT PEOPLE IN COURT

Bill Eddy
LCSW, ESQ

Eddy, Bill, 1948-
Managing High Conflict People in Court / by Bill Eddy
Includes bibliographical references

ISBN 978-1-936268-01-6

First printing: May 2008

Book design: Pierpoint-Martin

Publisher:
Published by HCI Press
www.hcipress.com

Printed in the United States of America

ABOUT THE AUTHOR

William A. ("Bill") Eddy is President of the High Conflict Institute, LLC, Scottsdale, Arizona, and Senior Family Mediator at the National Conflict Resolution Center in San Diego, California.

He is a Certified Family Law Specialist in California with fifteen years' experience representing clients in family court since 1993, and a Licensed Clinical Social Worker with twelve years' prior experience providing therapy to children, adults, couples, and families in psychiatric hospitals and out patient clinics.

He taught Negotiation and Mediation at the University of San Diego School of Law for six years. He provides seminars on mental health issues for judges, attorneys, and mediators, and seminars on law and ethics for mental health professionals. His articles have appeared in national law and counseling journals.

A recognized speaker in the United States and Canada, Bill Eddy has become an authority and consultant on the subject of high conflict personalities for collaborative professionals, employee assistance and human resource professionals, ombudspersons, healthcare administrators, college administrators, homeowners associations, and others.

Bill Eddy obtained his law degree in 1992 from the University of San Diego, a Master of Social Work degree in 1981 from San Diego State University, and a Bachelors degree in Psychology in 1970 from Case Western Reserve University. He began his career as a youth social worker in a changing neighborhood in New York City and first became involved in mediation in 1975 in San Diego. He considers conflict resolution the theme of his varied career.

Bill Eddy's website is www.HighConflictInstitute.com. His Curriculum Vitae is provided in the Appendices.

BOOKS AND COURSES BY BILL EDDY

"It's ALL YOUR Fault!", 12 Tips For Managing People Who Blame Others For Everything (2008)
HCI Press

High Conflict People in Legal Disputes (2006, 2008)
HCI Press

The Splitting CD: An Interview with Bill Eddy (2006)
Eggshells Press

Splitting: Protecting Yourself While Divorcing a Borderline or Narcissist (2004)
Eggshells Press

Working with High Conflict Personalities (2004, 2006) (A Six-Hour Internet Course for Mental Health Professionals at www.continuingEdCourses.net)

ABOUT HIGH CONFLICT INSTITUTE, LLC

High Conflict Institute LLC. was co-founded in 2008 by William A. ("Bill") Eddy, LCSW, Esq., and Megan L. Hunter, MBA, to provide education and resources to professionals handling High Conflict disputes.

After years of working with High Conflict disputes in many settings, Bill Eddy came to the conclusion that these disputes are not driven by complex issues, but by High Conflict People ("HCPs") with personality disorders or traits.

Based on Bill's three decades of experience and broad training in mental health, law and conflict resolution, he developed the High Conflict Personality Theory (the "HCP Theory"). He has been teaching the necessary skills for handling HCPs to professionals in a wide variety of settings: legal, workplace, healthcare, education, government, business and others throughout the United States and Canada.

Megan Hunter developed the concept of the High Conflict Institute, after working in the Administrative Office of the Court for the Supreme Court of Arizona. She has worked in the area of judicial training and family law issues for the past 13 years.

For more information about seminars and consultations go to www.HighConflictInstitute.com.

MANAGING HIGH CONFLICT PEOPLE IN COURT

Introduction

People with high-conflict personalities ("HCPs") are increasing in our society and in our courts. As litigants, they have a familiar pattern of high-intensity emotions, distortions of information, and self-defeating behavior. Their prolonged disputes are characterized by unchanging hostility, replacement of resolved issues with new unresolved issues, and lack of insight and behavior change. Judicial officers often refer to them as "frequent filers" who can't let go of the litigation process. They have many of the characteristics of Cluster B personality disorders.

This article describes general principles and suggestions for judicial officers to use in managing people with high-conflict personalities in any courtroom, with an emphasis on family court litigants. As explained below, approximately half of these cases appear to involve two or more parties who are HCPs, while the other half may be driven primarily by one HCP with the other party generally acting reasonably.

MANAGING HIGH CONFLICT PEOPLE IN COURT

1. An Increase in Personality Disorders

People who meet the diagnostic criteria of a personality disorder comprise at least 14.8 % of the general population, according to the largest study of this subject (over 43,000 subjects interviewed) sponsored by the National Institutes of Health and reported in the *Journal of Clinical Psychiatry* in July 2004 (Grant, 2004). Unfortunately, this study did not include Borderline, Narcissistic and Schizotypal Personality Disorders; although a follow-up study intends to include them in the next few years.

The Diagnostic and Statistical Manual of Mental Disorders of the American Psychiatric Association, in its current edition (DSM-IV-TR), indicates that Borderline comprises approximately 2% and Narcissistic and Schizotypal comprise less than 1% each of the general population (APA, 2000). Given that some individuals meet the criteria for two or more personality disorders, those with these disorders may represent between 15% and 18% of the United States general population.

The above study also indicates that these personality disorders appear in all groups and sectors of our society. However, there are slightly higher percentages in urban areas and in those with lower incomes and less education. People who were married or living-with-someone-as-if-married had slightly less incidence of these disorders, while those who were widowed, divorced, separated or never in a marital-type relationship had a slightly higher incidence. Each younger age group (65+, 45-64, 30-44, 18-29) had a higher presence of these disorders, which suggests that personality disorders are increasing in our society. Anecdotal evidence from judicial officers across the U.S. and Canada in the author's seminars also indicates this increasing presence, especially in self-representing ("pro se") litigants.

A study of 1124 divorcing families reported in 1994 indicated that 15% were engaged in "intense" legal conflict and an additional 10% were in "substantial" legal conflict 2 ½ years after filing for divorce in two California counties. (Johnston, 1994) In another study, also reported in 1994, two-thirds of 160 parents in high-conflict divorces met the criteria for personality disorders, while one-quarter had less severe maladaptive personality "traits." (Johnston, 1994) That study used the criteria from the Third Edition of the American Psychiatric Association's Diagnostic and Statistical Manual of Mental Disorders, which is currently in its Fourth Edition, Text Revision: DSM-IV-TR. (APA, 2000)

"Can we, just for a moment, Your Honor,
ignore the facts?"

2. An Attraction to Court Process

The DSM-IV-TR lists 10 specific personality disorders, in three clusters (A, B and C). The Cluster B personality disorders are generally identified as "high drama" and include Borderline, Narcissistic, Antisocial and Histrionic. Many of those with Cluster B personality disorders – or less severe "traits" – appear to have high-conflict personalities which frequently land them in our courts, either as plaintiffs endlessly pursuing exaggerated or unfounded claims, or as defendants who escalate conflicts into violence or other harmful behaviors.

This author believes that over the past fifteen years our courts have become a prime playing field for undiagnosed and untreated personality disorders. This is because the adversarial court process has a similar structure to their disorders, combined with increased media exposure of courtroom procedures and dramas during this same time period. Ironically, while practitioners and parties experienced in the adversarial court process are making a significant shift to alternative dispute resolution methods (arbitration, mediation, settlement conferences, private judges, collaborative law), those with high-conflict personalities (HCPs) have become attracted to the traditional litigation process, seeking "my day in court." The following comparison from the author's book *High Conflict People in Legal Disputes (2006)* shows a striking fit:

Charecteristics of HCPs	Charecteristics of court process
Life-time preoccupation: blaming others	Purpose is deciding who is to blame; who is "guilty"
Avoid taking responsibility	The court will hold someone else responsible
All-or-nothing thinking	Guilty or not guilty are usually the only choices
Always seeking attention and sympathy	One can be the center of attention and sympathy
Aggressively seeks allies in their cause	Can bring numerous advocates to court
Speaks in dramatic, emotional extremes	Can argue or testify in dramatic, emotional extremes
Focuses intensely on others' past behavior	Can hear and give testimony on others' past behavior
Punishes those guilty of "hurting" them	Courts are where our society imposes punishment
Try to get others to solve their problems	Try to get the court to solve their problems
Its okay to lie if they feel desperate	Lying (perjury) is rarely acknowledged or punished

Because the thought structure of HCPs and the adversarial court process are such a perfect fit, HCPs are at times effective at making innocent people look guilty, while at the same time with their desperate charm and aggressive drive they often succeed at looking innocent themselves. Many cases that appear to be two HCPs fighting are actually driven by only one party who successfully makes the other party look bad. (Friedman, 2004)

A survey of 131 family law attorneys in San Diego County, California, in 2006, indicated they believed that approximately half of the high-conflict cases in family court are driven by two HCPs, while the rest have only one HCP and a non-HCP opposing party—who has, perhaps, been "walking on eggshells" for years. (Eddy & Waldman, 2007, as yet unpublished)

3. Unconscious Behavior

Most people are aware of the general impact of their own behavior on others, and they continually adapt and change their behavior from experience to be more effective in their lives. However, a key characteristic of HCPs is that they are truly unaware of the effect of their own behavior on others. This is the key reason that HCPs make no effort to change their problematic behavior. They see their behavior as normal and necessary under the circumstances, based on their life experiences and perceptions. It is part of who they are – their personalities.

A judge may be tempted to ask an HCP in frustration: *"Can't you see what you're doing to your child?"* Yet, HCPs truly cannot see, just as a blind person cannot see. Their self-awareness has been impaired from traumatic life experiences or from never becoming sufficiently developed in early childhood.

The result of this lack of self-awareness is that HCPs are unconsciously preoccupied with relationship fears, such as that they will be abandoned or disdained by those around them – especially those in close relationships or positions of authority. Negative verbal feedback from those around them, no matter how well-intended, has minimal useful impact. Long lectures, angry confrontations, or sarcastic comments do not impact their life-long rigid thought processes and are simply interpreted as personal dislike or disrespect by the court. Direct negative feedback seems to escalate their defensive (and often self-defeating) behaviors and their sense of fear.

Fear appears to drive much of these parties use of the court process. They fear being controlled by the other party, so that making even the smallest concession may feel like an invitation to annihilation. They fear they will lose everything. Much of this is unconscious and may be based on life-long fears for those with personality disorders, such as fear of a "loss of self" or loss of a very shaky sense of internal control. Because fear of these losses feels so *unbearable*, these parties keep returning to court. (Stahl, 1999)

4. Difficulty Regulating Emotions

One of the most dramatic symptoms of Cluster B personality disorders is "emotional dysregulation" – an inability to recognize or control the intensity and appropriateness of one's own emotions. (Linehan, 1993) Those with these disorders truly do not know what they are feeling and what has "caused" their feelings. They are often distressed by their own feelings and behaviors, which they struggle to understand or automatically think someone else caused.

Most judicial officers have had litigants who cannot hold back their angry outbursts in the courtroom, or their impulsive desire to speak when it will only harm their case. Some litigants cannot contain their emotional responses to the court's feedback or decisions, and they run out of the courtroom before their hearings are over. Yet at other times, the same parties can be extremely respectful, charming and very positive. Their mood swings are unpredictable and can be highly distressing to those around them.

Over the past fifteen years, there has been a dramatic increase in research on the brain, including how different parts of the brain process different types of information and actions. While many parts of the brain are involved in processing emotions and behavior, some researchers have found it helpful to note the differences between the left and right hemispheres. Generally, the right hemisphere is considered most active in regard to intuition, art, gathering global information, a photographic memory, sensitivity to non-verbal social cues, and also negative emotions. Generally, the left hemisphere is largely responsible for our use of language, applying patterned responses to the right hemisphere's global information, linear analysis of detailed information, and positive emotions (calm, contentment). (Seigel, 1999; Goldberg, 2005)

Linking the two hemispheres is the "corpus callosum," which is the neuronal wiring system largely responsible for the flow of information back and forth. For example, the right hemisphere may take a snapshot of the environment, and quickly assume that one is in danger. This can trigger the fight or flight response. Then, the left hemisphere may analyze the snapshot more deeply and determine that a familiar safe person is in the room. The initial fear response may then be replaced by a sense of calm, a decreased heart rate and normal breathing.

Research suggests that many of those with borderline personality disorder may have suffered from child abuse, which can impair brain development and result in the development of an impaired or smaller corpus callosum. (Lawson, 2004) This would reduce their ability to integrate information between the two hemispheres and may account for their sudden changes between uncontrollable emotional responses at times, and very positive interactions at other times – as they abruptly switch back and forth from right to left hemisphere, rather than both working smoothly together. This may help explain why impulsive domestic violence and impulsive child abuse are often associated with borderline personality disorder.

Interestingly, a recent study also shows that boys with neurodevelopmental disorders (ADHD, learning disabilities, etc.) may have similar difficulty communicating between the two hemispheres. Girls in general have a larger corpus callosum than boys, which may explain why boys have these disorders four to five times as often as girls. Apparently, boys process most verbal information primarily in their left, logical hemisphere and are less attuned to the social, nonverbal cues of the right hemisphere that girls use more often by processing language information with both hemispheres. (Cox, 2006)

On the other hand, women and men with personality disorders (women have been identified by mental health professionals as the majority of those with borderline and histrionic personality disorders; men the majority of those with narcissistic and antisocial personality disorders) may be over-stimulated by these emotional and nonverbal right hemisphere cues. Because of their personality disorders, they may have difficulty accessing their left hemispheres when they are experiencing negative emotions. This means they may be less able to use their left hemisphere's logical and linear analysis capabilities, which can help in managing these negative emotions when they are happening.

The importance of this brain research to courtroom management is that some litigants may be truly unable to manage or process their emotions in a productive manner in the courtroom. This will impact the management methods described below.

5. Cognitive Distortions

One of the largest problems of those with personality disorders in conflict situations is their significant distortion of past events, current relationships and future expectations. Over the past thirty years, cognitive researchers (Burns, 1980; Beck, 1990) have identified several cognitive distortions, which are generally unconscious and distressing to the person. The following are examples of cognitive distortions (thinking distortions) in laymen's terms:

- *All-or-Nothing Thinking* - seeing things in absolutes, when in reality little is absolute

- *Emotional Reasoning* - assuming facts from feelings (I feel stupid, therefore I am)

- *Personalization* – taking personally unrelated events, or events beyond your control

- *Mental Filter* – picking out a single negative detail and dwelling on it

- *Fortune Telling* – believing that you know the outcome of events, when you cannot

- *Labeling* – eliminating the realities of life with broad, negative terms (dummy, failure)

- *Mind-reading* – believing that you know what other people are thinking or intending

- *Minimizing the Positive, Maximizing the Negative* - distorting reality to fit your biases

- *Overgeneralization* - drawing huge conclusions from minor or rare events

- *Wishful Thinking* – expecting positive outcomes from unrelated or negative behavior

- *Projecting* – blaming others for thinking, feeling or behaving in ways that you are actually thinking, feeling or acting but can't see in yourself because

- *Splitting* – seeing certain people as absolutely "all-good" or "all-bad," so that the all-good person is justified in extremely fearing, hating or hurting the all-bad person

Each of these cognitive distortions may be more or less severe for a particular person at a specific time. However, those with personality disorders tend to have chronic cognitive distortions.

All of us have "automatic thoughts," including cognitive distortions, based on what we have heard and experienced over a lifetime – good and bad. Most people check their automatic thinking with current reality-based information. Sometimes we discover that our automatic thoughts contain cognitive distortions, and we change our thinking and our behavior accordingly.

However, those with personality disorders tend to believe their cognitive distortions and act on them as though they were true. Because their thinking feels true (emotional reasoning), they accept that it is true. Instead of examining these automatic thoughts for cognitive distortions, they defend their cognitive distortions.

Typical cognitive distortions in court are:

- *"The other party is all bad with no redeeming features."*
(All-or-Nothing Thinking)

- *"My child is sad after visitation, so the father must have abused her."*
(Jumping to Conclusions)

- *"The judge knows what I am thinking."*
  (Mind-Reading)

- *"I know my wife is having an affair."*
  (Projection, if 'he' is having unconscious sexual thoughts)

- *"Either you (child, therapist, attorney, judge) are on my side or you are against me."*
  (Splitting – people are all good or all bad)

- *"I know the judge will rule in my favor, finally vindicate me and validate my viewpoint."*
  (Fortune-telling/Wishful-thinking)

Much of this distortion process seems to be the result of difficulty managing emotions between the hemispheres. Brain researchers have confirmed that the left hemisphere will fabricate facts to make sense out of an unknown or distressing situation. (Damasio, 1999) Researchers have determined that memories are continually altered by the emotions associated with them, by the frequency of their use, and by the social feedback one receives regarding the memory. (Seigel, 1999) Those with borderline personality disorder, in particular, have been identified as unconsciously distorting reality to fit their intense, unregulated emotions. (Linehan, 1993; Mason & Kreger, 1998)

In the legal setting, the author of this article uses the term "emotional facts" for much of what is contested in high-conflict court cases. A useful definition may be "emotionally generated false information accepted as true and appearing to require emergency action." (Eddy, 2006) While some of these emotional facts may be knowingly false statements, they appear primarily driven by deeper, unconscious emotions and cognitive distortions. *("I had to lie, otherwise my child would be in great danger with the other parent.")* Unfortunately, much of what appears to happen in cases with HCPs is a debate over who is sincere and telling the truth, when in fact much of the debate is over these emotional facts, which are not true, but honestly believed or sincerely believed to be necessary falsehoods.

6. What Can Be Done?

In dealing with HCPs, there are four primary areas that need to be regularly addressed: Bonding, Structure, Reality-Testing, and Consequences. For judicial officers, the following are some specific suggestions in each area. It is important to keep in mind that there are no magic formulas for handling HCPs or making them stop returning repeatedly to

"As precedent your Honor I offer the entire legal history of western civilization on CD ROM."

court. Some will always be unresponsive – because of the nature of their disorder, not because of your efforts. Judicial officers are encouraged to think in terms of using the following methods to contain or manage their high-conflict cases, rather than to unrealistically (and perhaps wishfully) expect them to go away.

6.1 Bonding

You may not believe that you have a bond (a strong relationship) with someone who spends 10 – 20 minutes in your courtroom. However, in their minds, HCPs have already formed or will form a strong relationship with you. In many ways, it is like a child's relationship with a parent. HCPs tend to have significant fantasies and cognitive distortions regarding their relationships with others – especially those in positions of authority.

They are very likely to fit your comments into their all-or-nothing categories of "People Who Care About Me" and "People Who Don't Care About Me." Remember the Splitting concept described above. Before an HCP can listen to what you say, he or she is trying to determine which category applies to you. All of your feedback and orders will be interpreted by the category of one who cares or one who doesn't care. While many judges believe and say that it is not their job to care about the parties, HCPs will behave differently depending on their perceived bond with you, and will pick up your non-verbal messages regardless. These litigants are very sensitive to whether you show more empathy than disrespect.

Therefore, what you do matters – and "bonding" with HCPs can be done very quickly. The idea is to develop a positive relationship. Avoid directly criticizing one or both parties. That will impair your ability to form a positive relationship, and you will escalate the HCP(s) to come back again and again to try to prove that you are wrong about them.

Instead, give them your E.A.R.: your Empathy, your Attention, and your Respect. While this may *feel* like the last thing you want to do, it costs you nothing (you can still give them consequences) and makes a world of difference to HCPs. This is all they really want. They have unfortunately learned dysfunctional ways of trying to get empathy, attention and respect. If you just give it to them, they don't have to fight to get it. It also role-models how they need to treat their children. Parents in family courts often repeat what judges say over and over again to themselves and sometimes to their children.

Examples of E.A.R.:

"Sir, I can really empathize with your desire to see the children more than the present schedule. I am paying serious attention to your concerns. I also do respect the efforts you have been making to have more contact with your child."

"Ma'am, I really wish I didn't have to sanction you $100 for bringing this inappropriate issue to court. I can empathize with your frustrations with this formal legal process. I have paid attention to your concerns, and I will continue to pay attention to your concerns, even though I may end up disagreeing with them and having to give you consequences. And I do respect the efforts you made to keep this out of court at first. Hopefully, I won't have to do this again. Now, good luck to you in the future."

Or use the One-Minute Scold: This technique is taken from John Bowlby's work in the 1950's and 1960's with children adopted at an older age, such as 5 or 6 years old. He found that children who were just sent to their rooms or otherwise punished were not bonding with their adoptive parents. They needed an intense interpersonal method of discipline, not a rejecting one.

His "one-minute scold" includes 30 seconds during which you raise your emotional level and explain your frustrations and disappointments with the person's *behavior.*

"I must tell you how frustrated and disappointed I am that you still are getting your daughter to school late on your custodial days. I remember specifically telling you that you had to fix this problem so it doesn't happen again. I am reducing your parenting time because this behavior has not changed. You need to find a way to plan ahead on the mornings you still have."

Then, the remaining 30 seconds you lower your emotional level and use a calming, soothing tone to say:

"And the reason I'm telling you this is that I want you to succeed. I believe that you can succeed at this. I have high hopes for you and you have shown me in other areas that you can succeed and make important changes [of course, do not say this unless it has been true]. So you have my sincere backing on this. I hope, if I see you again in my courtroom, that you will have good news of new behaviors and successes to tell me."

I have witnessed some judges using this type of approach, and it has been very effective. Parties who were upset became calm and almost tearful, upon hearing that the court really wants them to succeed. It may be especially useful in cases of frequently returning parties, so that they can leave the courtroom feeling calm, respected and cared about – regardless of the difficult decisions that have been made.

6.2 Structure

High conflict people are constantly distressed, and many are in a state of chaos and lack of focus. On the other hand, there are some who can be very focused, especially when they are angry and have tunnel vision – a common occurrence with many HCPs who go to court. In either case, if your courtroom and procedures are very predictable, HCPs will be less anxious and more rational. HCPs respond better to consistent policies regarding continuances, filing papers, who speaks when, and what is bad behavior. When the process is fairly predictable, their emotions are less on edge, allowing their rational thoughts to dominate.

- *Joint Statement of Issues:*

Before any hearing, it may help to have the parties write down a joint statement of issues. This focuses them on a positive task, and gets them thinking about the other party's point of view. It also helps structure the issues for the court. If they don't have attorneys and haven't agreed on such a statement, then ask them each to submit their separate written statement of the joint issues in neutral terms. With high conflict people, this forces them to think about the other party's viewpoint in a slightly more objective manner. This activates their logical thinking process, which often reduces their negative emotions. If they know this is expected from the start, then they may come in slightly more focused on problem-solving than on heated arguments about each other.

- *Tentative Rulings:*

If you have read the pleadings, it can help the parties by giving them a tentative ruling. Then encourage them to go out in the hallway and see if they can negotiate a settlement, before arguing the case. Tentative rulings often reduce HCPs' unrealistic fantasies of great success or total failure. The legal possibilities are so vast, that they often over-react at the start of the case and make extreme legal claims in an effort to protect themselves. The build-up to a hearing or trial emotionally escalates HCPs away from their rational thinking, so that tentative rulings can bring them back into focus and they can be more productive. They honestly do not know what is important, what is not; and what is likely to happen and what is not.

- ### *Expect Negotiations:*

It often helps to establish a routine of required negotiations prior to a hearing or after a tentative ruling. Then the HCP will know that negotiations are expected – if for no other reason than to look good to the court. After hearing a tentative ruling, the HCP is more likely to be realistic and his or her attorney or support person can help the HCP cope with his or her initial emotional reaction long enough to settle down and focus on serious settlement options. Research indicates that it takes at least 20 minutes to calm down after the fight or flight responses have been triggered, and adrenaline has surged through the body. Apparently, men especially benefit from physical activity to burn off the excess adrenaline, so that an opportunity to walk around for a few minutes after hearing difficult information may be constructive.

- ### *Small Steps:*

Interestingly, HCPs do better with more time to consider issues in smaller bites. They are generally not responsive to efforts to "hammer out an agreement." Many potentially high-conflict cases have been resolved by handling them in small parts over time. Since it takes them more time to process information (emotionally first, then rationally), this need for time to adjust should be a serious consideration in the structure of court hearings. However, this does not have to take a long time. What is most important is that there are small steps to consider, one at a time, rather than a flood of information which requires an immediate response while the HCP is emotionally overloaded.

- ### *Delayed Opinions:*

Likewise, after hearing highly distressed arguments by the parties, you may decide to take the matter under submission and release a written opinion. This can be helpful to the management of HCPs, because it may make it easier for them to cope during the hearing itself, knowing they do not have to control their emotional reaction to a potentially upsetting decision. It also allows the person to receive the decision in the company of their attorney or friends or family, with time to soothe the likely upset feelings. However, the written opinion should not be delayed more than a few days or a week, or the tension of waiting may build and become unmanageable for the HCP.

6.3 Reality-Testing

High-conflict disputes are almost always about the facts, not about the law. When one or both parties have a high-conflict personality, the dispute over the facts will never end, because it is really a dispute over perceptions – distorted perceptions. Since their cognitive distortions are unconscious, arguing with their logic is unproductive and locks them deeper into defending their "emotional facts" (which *really* do feel real to the HCP).

It helps to start out by lowering expectations of the entire legal process. Attached to this article is a "Handout" which can help in establishing realistic expectations, which can be freely copied and used. It also helps if there are opportunities for litigants to get realistic assessments of their cases by a neutral person as soon as possible. Many high-conflict cases go for months or years with preparations based on unrealistic assessments by HCPs, which their attorneys or other supporters reluctantly (or enthusiastically) pursue. An early neutral evaluation of the case may bring their unrealistic expectations into focus, and avoid months or years of totally unnecessary litigation.

During the case, it helps to emphasize that we all have different viewpoints, based on our different life experiences. Our viewpoints are also influenced by our emotions, and litigation can be very stressful on our emotions. It also helps to acknowledge that you, as the formal decision-maker, will never know all the facts. Only legally permissible information will be considered, so what they believe are their best facts and arguments may never be properly heard by the court. From time to time say, *"You might be right. I'll never know all of the facts. But I have to make a decision based on the evidence before me."*

Evidence still matters. Since HCPs speak in emotional, dramatic terms much of the time, it helps to ask: *"Can you give me a specific example of how that happened?"* It also helps to gently challenge unusual information. *"Are you sure about that? It sounds very unusual to me."* Share your skepticism of *"emotional facts,"* which could be cognitive distortions *"under the stress of the divorce,"* rather than intentionally inaccurate information.

Be particularly skeptical of intense emotions and information that could be related to their personality-based cognitive distortions:

* **Feeling "abandoned"** (typical preoccupation of borderlines):

    "He abandoned the children and me, he abandoned his responsibilities to our family, he abandoned our lifetime vows, he took all our money, he abandoned me for another..."

- **Feeling "disrespected"** (typical preoccupation of narcissists),

- **Feeling "controlled"** (typical complaint of antisocials), or

- **Feeling "ignored"** (typical of histrionics).

When they claim abuse with no supporting evidence, but it seems to be more about these key themes, you may be dealing with an HCP and their information may be unreliable on all issues.

On the other hand, HCPs can be good at spotting abuse and they also may have been abused. So avoid jumping to conclusions about personalities. Openly share your doubts and desire for more evidence. If you admit that you cannot be certain and that you have deep concerns either way, you will be more credible with both parties and their attorneys or support persons.

The results of our 2006 survey of 131 family law attorneys in San Diego County showed that the attorneys believed approximately two-thirds of child sexual abuse allegations in divorce cases were false (about half of those were considered honestly believed and about half were considered knowingly false). The same survey showed serious doubts about the accuracy of the facts underlying domestic violence allegations in approximately 40% of restraining order hearings. In this survey, attorneys also indicated that they believed the majority of batterers and child abusers had personality disorders, as well as the majority of those making false allegations. (Eddy & Waldman, 2006, as yet unpublished) Of course, it is important to note that these are attorneys' beliefs, not the results of formal evaluations by mental health professionals. Yet their beliefs are significant because of the large size of the sample (over 100) and the years of experience (more than 15 years average) of the attorney respondents.

Therefore, to be credible with attorneys and self-representing parties, no presumptions would seem appropriate in handling these cases, although temporary protective orders should always take precedence. Rather than having expensive investigations and court sanctions at the end of the process, it is better to avoid presumptions from the start so that these cases are not unnecessarily escalated. This does not need to interfere with making protective orders, but instead puts these orders in perspective. Often, for HCPs, the protective orders escalate the case into a prolonged battle over who is "all-good" and who is "all-bad." When courts take a more *openly questioning approach, while still making protective orders,* it reduces the effect of abuse issues tipping all the apparent power to one party or the other for the next year or two – which often triggers HCPs to develop a pattern of coming back to court on a regular basis.

For example, when an HCP brings allegations of abuse to court requiring emergency orders that restructure the family (restricted parent contact, residence exclusion orders, etc.) with little factual information, it may help to admonish and reassure both parties about the use of that information, such as:

> *To Party A: "You are telling me that your spouse has abused you and/or the children, and that I should order him [or her] to leave the residence. This information is very important to me and also very concerning. On the one hand, I want to tell you that you might be right about the events that you described, and my top priority is protecting people from harm. On the other hand, I want to warn you that if I find out later that this was false or recklessly exaggerated information, it could have negative consequences for you."*

> *To Party B: "If I find out that it is true and you, sir [or ma'am], are denying it, it could have negative consequences for you. So I am ready to proceed and make protective orders. I would encourage each of you to discuss this further with your attorneys [or whoever you talk to for advice] before the full hearing on this matter. I want as much useful information as possible to help me make realistic decisions that will affect your future."*

This type of approach avoids creating an "invalidating environment," which many HCPs experienced in childhood, especially borderlines (Linehan, 1993). An "invalidating environment" is one in which a child's parents ignore normal behavior and disbelieve or criticize the child for truthful statements. Instead, the child learns that dramatic and extreme behavior gets more attention, and that false statements receive more attention and credibility. When a truthful parent (or one who believes what he or she is thinking is true) is present in court and is forcefully told that he or she is lying or distorting, it "invalidates" that parent's experience and can devastate him or her, so that he or she no longer provides important information to the court, or keeps coming back to court to prove he or she is really an "okay" person.

It's better to tell the parties:

> *"You might be right: What you are saying may be truthful and accurate, and the other party may be totally inaccurate or purposefully misleading. I will never know for sure. So I don't want to disregard your concerns and statements, but at this point the other party appears to*

me to be more credible. Based on the evidence before me, I find that this particular state-
ment of yours is contradicted by the evidence and therefore not credible to me. Evidence may
exist that shows that this finding is incorrect, but I have not seen it. "

6.4 Consequences

Consequences are the best way to attempt to change the behavior of HCPs, as direct
criticisms have little impact since their inappropriate behavior is unconsciously driv-
en. In this regard, HCPs are much like addicts and alcoholics – it takes specific consequences to motivate specific positive behavior change. Fortunately, our courts have some
consequences which can be imposed. Unfortunately, they are very limited. Financial
sanctions and jail time may be motivating, but on their own they do little to change
long-term behavior. Small reductions in parenting time may be a realistic consequence
for inappropriate behavior in custody and access disputes. A combination of financial
consequences or legal restraints with some type of treatment is most effective with personality disorders and traits.

What is really necessary is a program of change. At present there are few individual
therapists trained in the effective treatment of personality disorders, but there is grow-
ing interest and hope. The most exciting news comes from Dialectical Behavior Therapy
(DBT) developed by Marsha Linehan, Ph.D., of the University of Washington in Seattle.
(Linehan, 1993) This approach emphasizes helping the client develop skills for managing
emotions, accepting oneself in the present, and taking action steps to improve one's daily
life in small steps. Other cognitive-behavioral therapies are also being used in individual
therapy (Beck, 2004) and as part of other treatment programs (substance abuse treatment, eating disorder treatment, batterers' treatment).

Ordering HCPs into treatment of some kind can be helpful, so long as it is not simply
supportive therapy that does not challenge the HCPs thinking and behavior. It is easy
for therapists to become overly sympathetic with HCPs, who are good at manipulating
people into taking care of them and taking their "side" in their daily conflicts. Therapists
who are knowledgeable about working with personality disorders or traits can be very
effective at assisting in positive behavior change. Finding out who is knowledgeable in
your area can make a great difference in the outcome.

When ordering therapy with an individual therapist, it is helpful to have specific goals.
In general, therapists are used to being client-centered and let the client set the goals.
However, when clients have personality disorders or less severe traits, they usually lack

the ability to set meaningful goals. Instead, they lack self-awareness and resist change, even when it would be beneficial. Therefore, it can help the therapist as well as the client to know clearly why therapy was ordered.

For example: *"To work on new ways to heal from the divorce." "To work on new ways to protect the children from her negative emotions about the other parent." "To look at his part in the parent conflicts and try new ways of communicating."* This helps the therapist work with the client on "new ways" of behaving, rather than just nurturing the client, focusing only on the client's feelings, or (as happens too often) just listening to the client vent about the other party. While keeping the content of the therapy sessions confidential, the court can later ask the party, if he or she returns to court: *"Tell me two or three new ways of doing things you have learned in your therapy?"*

7. CONCLUSION

No one handles these clients perfectly and there will always be some high-conflict individuals you simply cannot reach. There will always be some HCPs with such severe personality disorders that there will be no change or improvement. However, I believe that the majority of high-conflict cases can see improvement with effective handling by all professionals involved, even though the clients have personality disorders or traits.

The focus must be on managing (not eliminating) these cases, avoiding getting emotionally hooked, and maintaining a calm and confident demeanor which does not engage their uncontrollable emotions. These cases require extreme patience, structure, and support from colleagues. Yet, even with small amounts of success, many of these parties can be helped.

APPENDIX 1

TIPS FOR JUDICIAL OFFICERS
MANAGING THE HIGH CONFLICT CASE

Bonding

1. There may be one or two HCPs, so have relatively equal eye contact and comments

2. HCPs need to feel a positive connection with the court to feel secure and to cooperate

3. Empathize with their intense emotions, then focus on the task at hand

4. Remember: They are in distress, can't solve this themselves and truly need your help

5. Avoid getting emotionally hooked, because it's hard to be very emotional and rational

6. You know you're hooked when:

    *   You are suddenly angry
    *   You don't want to have eye contact
    *   You feel you have to argue with the HCP(s)
    *   You feel you don't have any choices

7. Use the One-Minute Scold, if appropriate:

    Emotional voice: 30 seconds about disappointment with behavior (not person)

    Soothing voice: 30 seconds about wanting to help person succeed and your belief that he or she can succeed at the next task

8. Regularly (and briefly) give them your E.A.R. statement:

    *   Empathy
    *   Attention
    *   Respect

9. Be educational (think of a young child who truly doesn't understand)

10. Praise their strengths and skills; help them save face

Structure

1. Remember: They are often in emotional chaos and need help focusing on next steps

2. Contain emotions (acknowledge feelings without opening them up)

3. Focus them on tasks (give them homework)

4. Reduce expectations of the court process

5. Encourage a joint statement of issues

6. Make detailed court orders; anticipate violations and build in consequences

7. Build in step-by-step expectations; use review hearings to keep on track

8. Don't work harder than they do (*Ask: What should we do about this?*)

Reality-Testing

1. When in doubt, safety first!

2. Explain your ambivalences about the evidence; ask for more information

3. Remember: HCPs have significant and unconscious cognitive distortions

4. Stay open-minded throughout the case; avoid presumptions about behavior

5. Tell the parties you will never know for sure

6. Don't create an *"invalidating environment"*: say it's *possible* they are correct

7. Ask for *specifics* to support their broad complaints and emotional conclusions

8. Expect lying, but recognize they may honestly believe their false statements

9. Avoid arguing with the party's logic

10. Focus on future decisions, based on where the evidence points you

Consequences

1. HCPs don't have insights from being criticized; they escalate instead

2. Consequences are better than criticisms

3. A credible threat of future consequences may be helpful

4. Court orders need consequences built in

5. Small sanctions are an excellent consequence

6. Changes in schedule may be best consequence for parenting problems

7. Cognitive-Behavioral Treatments can help (individual or group therapies)

8. HCPs need a long-term program of change, just like addicts/alcoholics

9. HCPs are motivated by consequences, just like addicts/alcoholics

10. Your positive comments can be a powerful motivator for these fragile parties

APPENDIX 2

THREE STAGES OF HIGH CONFLICT CASES

Starting the Case

1. From the start: reduce expectations of court process

2. Educate about limited decision-making based on admissible evidence

3. Educate about dangers of emotional reasoning driving a case

4. Threaten consequences for false or reckless statements

5. See Appendix 3, "Before You Go To Court" Handout

Managing the Case

1. Avoid getting emotionally hooked

2. Be matter-of-fact, rather than criticizing

3. Maintain a healthy skepticism throughout the case

4. Remind them it's not about who's the better person

5. Threaten consequences for continuous negative actions

6. Provide consequences when appropriate, but in a matter-of-fact manner

Ending the Case

1. High conflict cases often do not end, but may be contained

2. They may not accept the other party's ideas, but they often accept the same thing from a neutral person in authority

3. They need to participate in the final decisions, or they will not accept them

4. If they can tinker with it, then they may accept it, even though they may complain

5. If they feel respected by the Court, they may be able to let go

6. Saving face helps in letting go

APPENDIX 3

BEFORE YOU GO TO COURT

- Make Sure You Have Realistic Expectations

In Court, the judge or jury will never really know what is going on in your case. The Court's job is to decide narrow legal issues based on limited permissible evidence. Hearings and trials are mostly short and to the point. In real life, Court is not like most court cases on television or the movies – or even the news. Trials are rare, as most cases are resolved by hearings and/or settlement by agreement of the parties – often with the help of knowledgeable attorneys.

- Do Not Expect Validation or Vindication

The judge or jury does not decide your character as a person – or who has been "all good" or "all bad." In Court, it is often assumed that both parties have contributed to the problem, and that it is a matter of relative liability for whatever occurred. Today, many courts focus on problem-solving. Interpersonal complaints are often seen as "he said, she said," and the courts much prefer that these disputes be settled out of court.

- Avoid Emotional Reasoning

When people are upset, our perceptions can be distorted temporarily or permanently. Our emotions may cause us to jump to conclusions, view things as "all or nothing," take innocent things personally, fill in "facts" that are not really true, unknowingly project our own behavior onto others, and unconsciously "split" people into absolute enemies and unrealistic allies. This happens at times to everyone, so check out your perceptions with others to make sure they have not been distorted by the emotional trauma of the dispute and related events. Many cases get stuck in court for years fighting over who was lying, when instead it was emotional reasoning which could have been avoided from the start.

- Provide The Court With Useful Information

The judge or jury does not know you or your issues, except for the information that is properly submitted to the court. Make sure to provide important information, even if it is embarrassing. The court cannot sense the behavior of each party. If you feel you have been abused by another person, the court needs sufficient information to make helpful decisions. If you hold back on important information, it may appear that abusive incidents never occurred and that you are exaggerating or making knowingly false statements. If you are accused of actions you did not take, the court will not know this information is inaccurate or false unless you sufficiently inform the court.

- Be Careful About Un-verifiable Information

The accuracy of the information you provide to the court is very important. Based solely on what you say in declarations or testimony in court, the judge or jury may make very serious orders regarding the other party, yourself, and your finances. If it later turns out that you made false or reckless statements -- even if you were well-intentioned -- there may be negative consequences, such as sanctions (financial penalties) or other restrictions in your future actions. A legal history may be a liability in future employment, relationships and court cases.

- Try To Settle Out-Of-Court

Today there are many alternatives to going to court which can be used at any time in your case, including Mediation, Collaborative Law, Arbitration, negotiated agreements with attorneys, and settlement conferences assisted by a settlement judge. The expense for each of these is much less than for court hearings, trials, and prolonged disputes. You have nothing to lose, and you can still go to court afterwards if you do not reach a full agreement. By trying an out-of-court settlement, you can limit animosity and protect yourself and your family from the tension and cost of several months or years in court battles.

REFERENCES

American Psychiatric Association. (2000). *Diagnostic and Statistical Manual of Mental Disorders, Fourth Edition, Text Revision.* Washington, DC: American Psychiatric Association.

Beck, A. & Freeman, A. (2004). *Cognitive Therapy of Personality Disorders, Second Edition.* New York, NY: The Guilford Press.

Burns, D. (1980). *Feeling Good: The New Mood Therapy.* New York, NY: Morrow.

Cox, A. (2006). Helping Boys Cross the Communication Divide. *The Brown University Child and Adolescent Behavior Letter,* 22 (5): 1,3, May 2006.

Damasio, A. (1999). *The Feeling of What Happens.* New York, NY: Harcourt Brace & Company.

Eddy, W. (2006). *High Conflict People in Legal Disputes.* Calgary, AB: Janis Publications.

Friedman, M. (2004). The So-Called High-Conflict Couple: A Closer Look. *The American Journal of Family Therapy,* 32:101-117, 2004.

Grant, B. F., Hasin, D. S., Stinson, R. S., Dawson, D. A., Chou, S. P., Ruan, W. J., & Pickering, R. P. (2004). Prevalence, Correlates, and Disability of Personality Disorders in the United States. *Journal of Clinical Psychiatry,* 65:7, July 2004.

Johnston, J. (1994). High-Conflict Divorce. *The Future of Children,* 4:1, Spring/Summer 1994.

Lawson, C. (2004). Treating the Borderline Mother. *Family Treatment of Personality Disorders.* New York, NY: The Haworth Clinical Practice Press.

Linehan, M. (1993). *Cognitive-Behavioral Treatment of Borderline Personality Disorder.* New York, NY: The Guilford Press.

Goldberg, E. (2005). *The Wisdom Paradox.* New York, NY: Gotham Books.

Mason, P. & Kreger, R. (1998). *Stop Walking on Eggshells.* Oakland, CA: New Harbinger Publications.

Seigel, D. (1999). *The Developing Mind.* New York, NY: The Guilford Press.

Stahl, P. (1999). *Complex Issues in Child Custody Evaluations.* Thousand Oaks, CA: Sage Publications.

CURRICULUM VITAE

William A. Eddy, LCSW, JD
Attorney and Mediator
President, High Conflict Institute, LLC
7701 Indian School Road, Ste. F
Scottsdale, AZ 85251
Tel: (602) 606-7628 Fax: (602) 476-7349
www.highconflictinstitute.com

Education:

University of San Diego School of Law
J.D. received in May 1992
Randolph A. Read Law and Psychiatry Award

San Diego State University
M.S.W., Master of Social Work, May 1981

Case Western Reserve University
B.A., Psychology, May 1970

Professional Licenses:

Attorney and Counselor at Law: CA Bar #163236

- Licensed by Supreme Court of California (1992 to present)
- Licensed by United States District Court (1992 to present)

Licensed Clinical Social Worker: CA #LCS12258 (1986 to present)

Professional Certificates:

Certified Family Law Specialist, CA Bar Association (2003 to present)

Practitioner Member of Association of Conflict Resolution (1994 to present) (*Formerly Academy of Family Mediators and SPIDR*)

Credentialed Mediator by National Conflict Resolution Center (1993 to present) (*Formerly San Diego Mediation Center*)

Employment

President, High Conflict Institute, LLC (January 2008 to Present)

- Provide training and consultation to judges, attorneys, mediators, collaborative professionals, mental health professionals, and others regarding high conflict disputes involving high conflict personalities.

Senior Family Mediator (January 2005 to Present)

National Conflict Resolution Center (*Formerly San Diego Mediation Center*)

- Provide divorce mediation services for approximately 70 couples per year.

Attorney and Mediator, Sole Practitioner, San Diego, CA (1993 to 2007)

- Family Law and Mediation Practice: Handled over 500 cases as a family law attorney, over 900 divorce mediations, and 100 civil mediations, including Superior Court cases. Occasional Collaborative Divorce attorney, Special Master and Settlement Judge.

Adjunct Professor, Negotiation and Mediation Course, 7 Semesters (1997-2003)

- Interviewing and Counseling Difficult Clients (2000) University of San Diego School of Law

Psychotherapist (Clinical Social Worker) Counseling & Recovery Institute, San Diego, CA (1987 - 1992)

- Psychotherapy for chemically dependent, depressed and divorced adults, their children and families.

Psychotherapist (Clinical Social Worker) Mesa Vista Psychiatric Hospital, San Diego, CA (1985 - 1987)

- Family therapy and discharge planning for substance abuse and adolescent units.

Director, Seattle University Child Care Center, Seattle, WA (1981 - 1984)

- Directed program for 50 families with children ages 2 - 6; including some counseling.

Clinical Social Work Intern, Child Guidance Clinic, Children's Hospital, San Diego, CA (1980)

• Part-Time Family Therapist during MSW Training Program

Trainings As Presenter As of December 2007

MANAGING CONFLICT IN CUSTODY AND ACCESS CASES, National Judicial Institute, Alberta Education Seminar, Edmonton, Alberta (11/15/07)

HIGH CONFLICT INSTITUTE FOR FAMILY LAW PROFESSIONALS, Presenter for 2-day Institute in Dallas, TX (11/13-14/07) Sponsored by National Conflict Resolution Center and Family Law Solutions.

HIGH CONFLICT INSTITUTE FOR FAMILY LAW PROFESSIONALS, Presenter for 2-Day Institute in New Orleans, LA (11/8-9/07) Sponsored by National Conflict Resolution Center and Family Law Solutions.

HANDLING HIGH CONFLICT PEOPLE IN COLLABORATIVE PRACTICE, Pre-Conference Institute, International Academy of Collaborative Professionals, Toronto, Ontario (10/26/07)

HIGH CONFLICT PERSONALITIES IN ALTERNATIVE DISPUTE RESOLUTION, Ontario Bar Association – ADR Section, Toronto, Ontario, Canada (10/25/07)

HOW TO DEAL WITH HIGH CONFLICT OPPOSING PARTIES AND COUNSEL, Alaska Bar Association, Anchorage, AK (10/17/07)

HIGH CONFLICT INSTITUTE FOR FAMILY LAW PROFESSIONALS, Presenter for 2-day Institute in Philadelphia, PA (10/4-5/07) Sponsored by National Conflict Resolution Center and Family Law Solutions.

HIGH CONFLICT INSTITUTE FOR FAMILY LAW PROFESSIONALS, Presenter for 2-Day Institute in Chicago, IL (9/27-28/07) Sponsored by National Conflict Resolution Center and Family Law Solutions.

HANDLING IMPAIRED JUDICIAL OFFICERS, Association of Judicial Disciplinary Counsel, San Diego, CA (7/26/07)

HANDLING HIGH CONFLICT PERSONALITIES IN WORKPLACE DISPUTES Employee Assistance Personnel Association, San Diego, CA (7/25/07)

HANDLING HIGH CONFLICT PERSONALITIES IN HEALTHCARE DIS-PUTES Navy Medical Center San Diego, San Diego, CA (6/27/07)

DEALING WITH HIGH CONFLICT PERSONALITIES IN THE COURT-ROOM, 2007 Arizona Judicial Conference, Arizona Supreme Court, Scottsdale, AZ (6/21/07)

HANDLING HIGH CONFLICT PERSONALITIES IN WORKPLACE DIS-PUTES, Influential Women Executives' Group, Orange County, CA (5/11/07)

HANDLING HIGH CONFLICT PEOPLE IN COLLABORATIVE DIVORCE, New Mexico Collaborative Practice Symposium, Albuquerque, NM (5/5/07)

HANDLING PERSONALITY DISORDERS IN FAMILY COURT CASES, American Bar Association Family Law Conference, Monterey, CA (4/28/06)

CALIFORNIA FAMILY LAW JUDGES AND MEDIATORS ANNUAL INSTI-TUTE, Annual Judicial Institute, Judicial Council of California, San Francisco, CA (4/20/07)

HANDLING PERSONALITY DISORDERS IN FAMILY COURT CASES, Minnesota Interdisciplinary Committee on Divorce, Minneapolis, MN (4/13/07)

HIGH CONFLICT INSTITUTE FOR FAMILY LAW PROFESSIONALS, Presenter for 2 ½ - day Institute in Phoenix (3/8-10/07)

"I Won't Go!" A NEW LOOK AT PARENTAL ALIENATION, Attorney-Therapist Interface Luncheon, San Diego County Bar, CA (2/23/07)

HIGH CONFLICT PERSONALITIES IN COLLABORATIVE DIVORCE, Collaborative Divorce Solutions of Orange County, Orange, CA (2/13/07)

HANDLING BORDERLINES AND NARCISSISTS: 7 SKILLS FOR FAMILY COURT PROFESSIONALS, Association of Family and Conciliation Courts, AFCC – CA, Annual Conference, San Francisco, CA (2/10/07)

COGNITIVE ISSUES IN MARITAL AND DIVORCE CONFLICT, Sharp Mesa Vista Hospital Grand Rounds, San Diego, CA (11/18/06)

HANDLING PERSONALITY DISORDERS IN FAMILY COURT CASES, Judicial Council of California, Regional FCS Training, Sacramento, CA (11/17/06)

HANDLING PERSONALITY DISORDERS IN FAMILY COURT CASES, Alaska Court System Professionals Custody Training, Anchorage, AK (11/2/06)

YOU AND YOUR PRACTICE: HANDLING HIGH CONFLICT PERSONALITIES, Alaska Bar Association, Anchorage, AK (11/1/06)

BORDERLINES AND NARCISSISTS: 7 SKILLS FOR DISPUTE RESOLVERS, Association for Conflict Resolution Annual Conference, Philadelphia, PA (10/25/06)

HIGH CONFLICT PERSONALITIES IN COLLABORATIVE DIVORCE, International Academy of Collaborative Professionals Annual Conference, San Diego, CA (10/14-15/06)

DEALING WITH HIGH CONFLICT PERSONALITIES
Navy Medical Center Administrators and Doctors, San Diego, CA (10/13/06)

DEALING WITH HIGH CONFLICT PEOPLE, Walters HOA Management Company, San Diego, CA (10/3/06)

CHILD SEXUAL ABUSE AND DOMESTIC VIOLENCE: ASSESSING TRUE & FALSE REPORTS, Flagstaff Family Court Professionals, Flagstaff, AZ (9/29/06)

DEALING WITH DIFFICULT PEOPLE IN MODERN TIMES, Homeowners Association Board Retreat, Rancho Santa Fe, CA (8/11/06)

WORKING WITH BORDERLINES AND NARCISSISTS
National Organization of Forensic Social Workers, Chicago, IL (7/19/06)

MANAGING HIGH CONFLICT PERSONALITIES IN LEGAL DISPUTES, Utah State Bar Convention, Newport Beach, CA (7/13/06)

HIGH CONFLICT PERSONALITIES IN FAMILY COURT LITIGATION, Arizona State Bar Convention, Family Law Section, Phoenix, AZ (6/16/06)

CHILD SEXUAL ABUSE AND DOMESTIC VIOLENCE: ASSESSING TRUE AND FALSE REPORTS, Arizona Court Professionals, Phoenix, AZ (6/8/06)

HANDLING HIGH CONFLICT PEOPLE IN BUSINESS, AT WORK & AT HOME, Public Seminar Emphasized Human Resource Professionals, Alberta, Canada (5/16/06)

PRESENTATION ON HIGH CONFLICT LITIGANTS
Family Court Judges, Queen's Bench, Alberta, Canada (5/15/06)

HANDLING HIGH CONFLICT PERSONALITIES IN & OUT OF FAMILY
COURT, Family Court Counselors, Commissioners, Attorneys, Alberta, Canada
(5/15/06)

LAW AND ETHICS 2006 – CONFIDENTIALITY UPDATE
Society for Clinical Social Work, San Diego, CA (5/5/06)

LAW AND ETHICS 2006, Kaiser Dept. of Psychiatry and Addiction Medicine, San
Diego, CA (4/18/06)

WORKING WITH HIGH CONFLICT PERSONALITIES
The Ombudsman Association, La Jolla, CA (4/2/06)

LAWYERS ON THE CUTTING EDGE OF ADR, Loyola Law School Center for
Conflict Resolution, Los Angeles, CA (3/17/06)

MINEFIELDS OF MALPRACTICE: HOW TO AVOID GETTING SUED, American Mental Health Alliance, Clinical Social Workers, San Diego, CA (10/21/05)

HANDLING PERSONALITY DISORDERS IN FAMILY COURT LITIGATION,
Arizona Domestic Relations Judicial Conference, Phoenix, AZ (10/5/05)

DATA ON PERSONALITY DISORDERS AMONG FAMILY COURT DISPU-
TANTS and PROFESSIONAL SPLITTING IN HIGH CONFLICT DISPUTES,
Association for Conflict Resolution Annual Conference, Minneapolis, MN (9/30/05)

ASSESSING PREVALENCE OF PERSONALITY DISORDERS IN HIGH-CON-
FLICT FAMILY COURT CASES, International Congress on Law & Mental Health,
Paris, France (7/7/05)

MANAGING LITIGANTS WITH PERSONALITY DISORDERS, Kentucky Family
Court Judges, 2005 Judicial Conference, Lexington, KY (6/28/05)

HIGH CONFLICT PERSONALITIES MEET COLLABORATIVE DIVORCE,
Coalition for Collaborative Divorce, Los Angeles, CA (6/11/05)

ENDING HIGH CONFLICT CASES, Panel Discussion with Family Court Judges,
Certified Family Law Specialists Summer Seminar, San Diego, CA (6/4/05)

HANDLING BORDERLINES AND NARCISSISTS: 7 SKILLS FOR MEDIA-TORS, Utah Council on Conflict Resolution, Salt Lake City, UT (5/10/05)

WORKING WITH NARCISSISTS AND BORDERLINES, New York State Council on Divorce Mediation, Saratoga Springs, NY (5/6/05)

HIGH CONFLICT PERSONALITIES: MANAGING THEIR EFFECT ON FAM-ILY DISPUTES, Alberta Family Mediation Society, Calgary, Canada (4/29/05)

WORKING WITH HIGH CONFLICT PERSONALITIES
The Ombudsman Association, Atlanta, GA (4/10/05)

MINEFIELDS OF MALPRACTICE: HOW TO AVOID GETTING SUED, Society For Clinical Social Work, San Diego, CA (4/1/05)

DEALING WITH HIGH CONFLICT PERSONALITIES
Navy Medical Center Administrators, Doctors and Staff, San Diego, CA (1/28/05)

HOW TO DEAL WITH HIGH CONFLICT PERSONALITIES, Sixth Judicial Dis-trict Family Mediation Program and Mediation Services of Eastern Iowa, IA (1/19/05)

WORKING WITH BORDERLINES AND NARCISSISTS: 7 SKILLS FOR DIS-PUTE RESOLVERS, Association for Conflict Resolution, 2004 Annual National Conference, Sacramento, CA (10/1/04)

HIGH CONFLICT PERSONALITIES IN FAMILY LAW PRACTICE, Foothills Bar Association, El Cajon, CA (8/10/04)

HANDLING HIGH CONFLICT PERSONALITIES IN CUSTODY DISPUTES, Annual Custody Evaluators Training, San Diego Volunteer Lawyers Project (7/17/04)

PARENTAL PSYCHOPATHOLOGY, Judicial Council of California, Family Court Services Southern Regional Training Institute (9/20/02)

LAW AND ETHICS FOR CLINICAL SOCIAL WORKERS
National Association of Social Workers, California Chapter (9/19/02)

LAW AND ETHICS FOR MENTAL HEALTH PROFESSIONALS, Riverside County Department of Mental Health Staff (8/27/02)

HIGH CONFLICT PERSONALITIES: Understanding & Resolving Costly Disputes, Association for Conflict Resolution, 2002 Annual National Conference (8/21/02)

CONFIDENTIALITY: WHAT THERAPISTS AND MEDIATORS NEED TO KNOW, San Diego County Bar Association, Attorney-Therapist Luncheon (4/27/01)

HANDLING CASES WITH PERSONALITY DISORDERS
San Diego Chapter, Society of Professionals in Dispute Resolution (7/10/00) and San Diego Mediation Center Staff and Volunteers (4/26/00)

BORDERLINE PERSONALITIES IN COURT AND MEDIATION, San Diego County Bar Association, Attorney-Therapist Luncheon (2/25/00)

SEMINAR ON HANDLING DIFFICULT CLIENTS
Miller & Associates, Criminal Defense Firm, Santa Monica, CA (6/12/99)

DIVORCE MEDIATION TRAINING, Volunteer Lawyer's Project, San Diego County Bar Assoc. (7/18/98, 7/25/98)

WORKSHOP PRESENTER, Speaker on Services for Middle Income Clients, California State Bar Convention (Fall 1997)

TRAINER, "Assessing Child Sexual Abuse Allegations in Divorce Cases", Seminar Presentations to Child Protective Services Staff (1996-1997)

MODERATOR AND ORGANIZER, "Current Issues in Divorce Mediation", San Diego County Bar Association Panel Presentation (Spring 1995)

GUEST LECTURER, Law & Family Therapy Course, USD School of Law (1994 - 1995), Mediation Course, Thomas Jefferson School of Law (1994 - 1995)

SEMINARS FOR THERAPISTS , "Legal Issues in Divorce" "Mediating Custody and Visitation Issues" (1993-1996) Law and Mediation Office of William A. Eddy, San Diego, CA

STAFF CONFLICT RESOLUTION TRAININGS, Hemophilia Foundation, Oakland, CA Fall 1993, County Mental Health Hospital, San Diego, Summer 1987, Mesa Vista Psychiatric Hospital, San Diego, Spring 1987

Trainings Attended:

Numerous National, State and Local Conferences and Seminars on Dispute Resolution, Family Law and Clinical Social Work (1980 - Present)

Professional Associations:

California State Bar Association
International Academy Of Collaborative Professionals
International Academy Of Law And Mental Health
National Association Of Social Workers
National Organization Of Forensic Social Workers
Society For Clinical Social Work
Association Of Family And Conciliation Courts
Association For Conflict Resolution (ACR)
San Diego Collaborative Family Law Group
San Diego County Bar Association
Southern California Mediation Association

Publications:

MANAGING HIGH CONFLICT PERSONALITIES IN COURT, Article Specifically for Judges, Janis Publications, Calgary, Canada (2007)

HIGH CONFLICT PEOPLE IN LEGAL DISPUTES
Janis Publications, Calgary, Canada (2006)

THE SPLITTING CD: An Interview with William Eddy,
Author of SPLITTING, Eggshells Press, Milkaukee, Wisconsin (2006)

Handling High Conflict Personalities in Family Mediation, ACResolution Quarterly Magazine of the Association for Conflict Resolution, Summer 2005, Washington, DC.

SPLITTING: Protecting Yourself While Divorcing a Borderline or Narcissist, 150 page manual for clients in difficult divorces, and their therapists and attorneys.
Eggshells Press, Milwaukee, Wisconsin (2004)

HIGH CONFLICT PERSONALITIES. Self-published, (2003). Re-issued as High Conflict People in Legal Disputes by Janis Publications (2006)

How Personality Disorders Drive Family Court Litigation,
VOIR DIRE, Magazine of the Solano County Bar Association, March/April 2000.

Dealing with Difficult Clients, CALIFORNIA LAWYER, Jan. 1999, p. 33.

YOUR COUNSELOR AT LAW Newsletter (1997 - 2005)

Negotiating Your Divorce, 70-Page Booklet, Self-Published 1997

Proposed Family Court Protocol for Cases Involving Sexual
Abuse Allegations, co-authored with William M. Benjamin, CFLS, Unpublished
60-page document submitted to San Diego Family Court judges, psychologists, and
related agencies (1997)

Mediating Economic Issues in Divorce: An Ethical Debate in Three Acts, 31 FAMILY
AND CONCILIATION COURTS REVIEW 354 (July, 1993)

Working With Addicted Parents, THE CONNECTION: Newsletter for   National
CASA Association, Advocates for Abused Children (1993)

Motivating Substance Abusing Parents in Dependency Court, 43 JUVENILE & FAM-
ILY COURT JOURNAL 11 (1992)

ON-TARGET PARENTING: A SELF-TRAINING MANUAL FOR RECOVER-
ING PARENTS, Lead author, Self-published (1991, 2000)

Couples in Recovery: Four-Stage Approach for Intimacy Restoration, FOCUS: EDU-
CATING PROFESSIONALS IN FAMILY RECOVERY (July 1989)

Internet Trainings:

"Its All Your Fault" – Working with High Conflict Personalities (July 2004 to Present)
www.ContinuingEdCourses.net, 6-Hours of CEUs for Mental Health Professionals